FIFTY SHADE
BY PHIL TO

D1650346

Like Phil on Facebook: Facebook.com/SuchaNiceGuy
Follow Phil on Twitter: @PhilTorcivia
Author website: Torcivia.com

Nothing in this book is true except my desire to cover my ass with this statement.

Cover designed by Anna V. Chastain of ChastainGraphics.com
Copy editing by Marguerite Walker II
Author photo by Micaela Malmi of EpicPhotoJournalism.com
Copyright ©2012 Phil Torcivia
ISBN: 147817286X
ISBN-13: 978-1478172864

CHAPTER ONE

By the time a man realizes that maybe his father was right,
he usually has a son who thinks he's wrong.
- Charles Wadsworth

I'm playing catch with my teenage son. He has his mother's blond hair. It's a typical July day in San Diego—warm, bright sunshine, and not a cloud in the sky. The only sounds are distant birds and the slap of baseball against mitt. *Little stinker has quite an arm.*

"No curve balls," I warn.

"I know. So, Pop," he asks as he hurls a four-seamer.

BZZZT, CRACK

Ouch.

"Yes?"

"I've been kind of seeing this girl at school."

"Seeing her or *seeing* her?" I pry as I toss the ball back a little harder.

PFFFT, SLAP

Not bad for sixty-seven. The old man still has it.

"You know, *seeing* her. Anyway, I was at her house last night, helping with calculus."

"Uh huh."

BZZZT, CRACK

"Her parents called her downstairs, so I did some exploration."

"And, what did you find?"

PFFFT, POP

"Well, since you're always warning me to avoid bedside tables, that was the first place I looked."

Oh, Jesus.

"And?"

3

"What's a butt plug?"

BZZZT, DINK, BONK — Curve ball, square in the nuts.

"Arrggh!"

I double over and feel as though my balls have shot out my ears.

"Honey. Wake up."

Who's shaking me?

"Mormon. Hey."

Oh, it's Bea.

"You had a bad dream, sweetie."

I check my package. All good. "Phew, that was a strange one."

"Tell me."

"I was playing catch with our son."

"Really? We haven't determined that it's going to be a boy, have we?"

"Well ..."

"OK, I'll play along. What did he look like?"

"A cross between Wayne Gretzky and the most beautiful woman in the world," I tease as I boop her nose and give her a kiss.

"Aw. And, his name?"

"Pippino."

"What?"

"Pippino. If we have a boy, that has to be his name," I state matter-of-factly.

"Ha, ha. You're silly."

"I'm not kidding. It's an Italian tradition. My first son must be named after my father, Pippino Silveri."

"No freaking way."

Is she serious?

"Yes, freaking way. I'll wrestle you for it," I say as I attack her. She giggles. "How do you manage to smell so good in the morning?"

"Don't change the subject, mister. Our son will not be named Pippino."

"Resistance is futile," I warn as I tug down on the waistband of her pajamas. "Do you hear that, Pippino?" I speak into her pelvis with my fake Italian accept. "You mamma, she's ashamed of-a you name."

"I think it's going to be a girl, anyway."

"Ah, Pippina!"

We laugh and wrestle, which naturally turns into morning sex. *No better way to start the day.* I'm thankful her morning sickness subsided, but I never realized women get hornier when pregnant. I'm definitely going to need assistance.

CHAPTER TWO

I love you, not only for what you are, but for what I am when I am with you. – Roy Croft

After good-morning nookie in my lover's condo, Bea hits the shower and I hit eggs on the side of an omelet pan. Once again, I'm derailed by the clinking of spoon against coffee mug. *The beast rises.*

"Top o' the morning to you, Ms. Aspinwald," I greet and bow.

"French toast."

"Huh?"

"I'd like French toast with cinnamon butter."

"Wouldn't you prefer *blue*berry muffins with a side of rabbit?" I sneer. I can hardly look at her since she defiled my glove.

"You do realize, Blobber, that this wedding isn't going to happen."

"It most certainly *is* going to happen. Didn't you get the invitation? This Saturday, Coronado Beach, noonish. Guests are encouraged to bring covered plates. I could sign you up for deviled eggs."

"Chris is a powerful man. I don't know if you're more brave or stupid ... I'm betting on stupid."

"You know dillweed has a girlfriend, right? Annie, I believe, was her name. Innocent thing with horrible taste in men."

"She's insignificant," Grandma sniffs as she pushes her reading glasses up her nose and stares at printed pages. "Do you know what this is, Blobber?"

"An excerpt from my blob?"

"Five forty five."

"Ah, it's your weight analysis," I respond while dipping bread in egg batter.

"It's your credit score."

Nosy little nit.

"Right. So?"

"You're behind on mortgage payments and you have four maxed-out credit cards."

"I also have a hairy mole on my ass," I respond while glaring at her.

"My granddaughter will soon realize you're marrying her to get your hands on my money. She'll dispose of you like dryer lint."

"I'm marrying her because I love her, and I'll gladly sign a pre-nup."

"Why don't you accept the offer from Chris, pay off your debts, and find a more appropriate mate—perhaps one with four legs."

"You two will never buy me off. Stop wasting your time."

"Warm up my coffee, and flip those before they burn."

I endure breakfast with the beast as I hear the shower turn off and wait for my love to rescue me.

"I must admit, you're a decent cook. I could put in a word for you at Denny's," Grandma remarks.

"How kind of you."

As Bea emerges from the bedroom in her silk robe, Grandma rises to leave. Naturally, she places my credit report in front of Bea on her way out.

"Have a wonderful morning. Bea, your future ex isn't a bad cook at all. He'll make someone a nice housewife someday," Grandma remarks as she exits.

"You made her breakfast? You're such a sweetie," Bea compliments as she crumbles the credit report, tosses it in the garbage, and checks the pan. "Ooh, French toast. Are these for me?"

"They are."

"And, I see you found the syrup," she teases as she dangles Mrs. Butterworth between her thumb and index finger. "I love syrup."

"Do you know what I'm going to do with that syrup later?"

"Pancakes?"

I take the bottle from her, squeeze a dot on my left index finger, and place it in her mouth. She sucks the tip, teasingly. I slide my finger down her chin, over her neck, and down her chest, parting her robe as I do. Bea tips her head back. I squeeze a bit more between her breasts and let it run a bit before catching the sugary stream with my tongue and planting a sweet kiss on her soft lips.

"I'm going to coat you and lick you to nirvana."

CHAPTER THREE

*In the arithmetic of love, one plus one equals everything,
and two minus one equals nothing. – Mignon McLaughlin*

On my way home, Bea's assistant, Eric, calls to invite me to
lunch. He refuses to tell me his motive over the phone.
*Maybe I can scarf more of those little yellow pills to help
keep up with my sexual dynamo.*

I get a few more blog entries done and meet Eric at the
San Diego County Fair. *Hmm, beer battered chocolate
covered bacon for lunch? Sure, why not? You only die once.* I
hope he's not a fan of rides, as my stomach has never
appreciated them.

"Big E, what's happening?"

"Good to see you, Mormon," he greets while giving me the
handshake, shoulder-bump man-hug." Let's hit the food
court. I'm starving."

"Me, too."

"So, I wasn't sure if Bea told you, but she has asked me to
walk her down the aisle Saturday, and I wanted to make
sure you're cool with that."

"Dude, of course I am. You know, she rarely speaks about
her parents."

"She was twelve when they had the accident. Her
grandmother and various nannies raised her."

"Well, she turned out perfectly crazy, and I'm absolutely
crazy about her. I just wish there were some way to win over
Grandma and make Chris disappear."

"I'm sure it will work out. Love conquers all, Mormon.
Ooh, and speaking of love," Eric beams as a handsome
fellow approaches; "here comes my man, Daniel."

We greet and stroll around the Fair, sampling the artery cloggery that abounds.

"So, gentlemen, I'd like to enlist your help in a stunt I'm planning. Bea is having a girls' night with her friends on Thursday. I want to surprise them with something. Should I hire a male stripper?"

"Wait. Wasn't she on stage for your party?" Eric asks.

"Indeed she was."

"Then you must return the favor," Daniel adds.

Ha! No fucking way.

"Yes, dress up in a police uniform and jump out of a cake," Eric teases.

"Right."

"I'm serious. It would be hysterical."

"It would be traumatizing. I'm fifty. I *eat* cake."

"Oh my god, I still have that uniform from the Pride Parade. It comes with handcuffs, too," Daniel offers.

"Perfect," Eric cheers, "and you two are similar size. You must, Mormon. Come on. We'll both be there to provide oral, I mean *moral* support."

"Seriously?"

"Please," they chime, in stereo.

"Fine. Fuck it. I'll chug half a bottle of tequila and do it."

"I'll arrange for the cake and bring Daniel's costume to work with me tomorrow," Eric insists.

"Can't believe I'm going to do this. Will Grandma be there?"

"No, Thursday is bingo night at The Rock Church. She'd never miss that."

"Phew. Now I need a favor from you, Eric."

"Anything."

"Got any more of those pain-thrillers Bea borrowed from you?"

"Indeed I do," Eric agrees.

"Might I have a handful for the honeymoon? I'm probably going to need all the help I can get."

"Of course."

The three of us enjoy the sights, then go our separate ways. I brainstorm ideas to make my emergence from pastry more amusing. This calls for restraints, a whip, and the biggest, blackest strap-on I can find. *Hustler Store, here I come.*

CHAPTER FOUR

Love is friendship set on fire. – Jeremy Taylor

I'm greeted at the door of the Hustler Store by a lovely young lady wearing an apron. She asks if I need help. *Lots.* Do I dare ask about the apron? *No.*

It's a vast store, with stripper wear on the first floor and stairs leading up to the loft of kinkery.

"My name is Nelly. Do you have anything special in mind?"

"I don't even know where to begin, Nelly."

"Well," she asks, "is it for a man or a woman?"

"For this man's woman."

"Excellent. What does she enjoy?"

"Overtime goals and zucchini."

"Um ..."

"Right. You can see my predicament."

She leads me along a wall of dildos and vibrators. I'm not one to blush, but this place has me crimson.

"What does this do?" I ask while attempting to read the price without touching the U-shaped device.

"Ah, this one is very popular. You have a good eye, sir." She sounds like she's selling me a BMW. "This vibrator stimulates the woman, both inside and out."

I stand perplexed.

"Her clitoris and her G-spot."

"Of course. I'd like one in purple. Oh, and someone stole my Fukuoku Glove, so I'll need one of those too—in black, please. Anything else you can recommend?"

"Lotions?"

"Do you have bacon-flavored?"

"..."

"Kidding. Something minty will do."

15

"Excellent. Anything else? Perhaps more advanced devices for the adventuresome?"

"Bring it."

She leads me over to the corner with triangular dildo-ish toys and strings with different sized beads and a ring that reminds me of the merry-go-round ride of my childhood.

"Do you know what these are?"

"Dog toys?"

"No, silly, these are for anal play." *Ouch.* "These are butt plugs and these are anal beads. They'll both go well with your minty lube. Have you used either before?"

"Of course, I have. I'm a skilled plugologist."

"Great. Then, you'll require his and hers."

"Whoa, Nelly—only hers."

"Ever tried it?"

"No."

"How about a pinky?" she gestures.

"What?"

"You know, during a blowjob. It heightens the sensation."

"Exit only."

"Don't be like that. It doesn't mean you're gay. The anus is quite sensitive and erogenous."

"Yes, it is," adds a boy-stander I'm unaware is standing by me. "You must try the beads too. They all go in except the ring, and just when you're ready to pop, have your lover yank them out with the ring. Heavenly!"

My virgin butt hole puckers as I try to digest their suggestions.

"Fine. Double bag them. Here's my card."

Lovergirl has me outmatched, but I plan to prove I can hang. I'll whip out my new arsenal and wear her ass (*tee, hee*) out before she leaves for her girls' night. *Shit! I almost forgot.*

"I also need a big black strap-on."

"Will the Cockasaurus Rex do?" she asks while dangling something resembling a toasted Genoa Salami in front of me.

"I believe it will."

CHAPTER FIVE

Let there be such oneness between us, that when one cries,
the other tastes salt. – Rossabelle Believe

Bea accepts my offer to cook dinner—stuffed artichokes and filet kabobs. When she arrives, I'm on my second glass of wine. I've left the sex toys in the plain paper bag between our place settings.

"What's in the bag?"

"Dessert, my love. No peeking!"

"You're no fun."

"Oh, just you wait."

"I'll go upstairs and freshen up. Be right back."

I continue cooking with wine, my unconventional way. Sure, I'm a little heavy on the garlic salt, but it makes everything better, as long as both lovers partake.

"Sweetie?"

"Yes."

"Can you come up here a minute?"

"Sure." *Uh, oh. What did she find?*

When I step into my master bath, she's wearing one of my button-downs and her lace panties, standing sideways in front of the full-length mirror.

"Look!" she glows, showing the first signs of a baby bump.

"Hm. I've got two words for you: salad bar."

"Hey."

"Light beer?"

"Stop it."

"Can you feel that lunch burrito kicking?"

"Ha, ha. Not yet. I'm just over four months, so this is about right. No more top buttons for me," she pouts.

"So cute. Can I take a picture and post it as little Pippino's first update on Facebook?"

"No, Gordon will not have a Facebook account until he is sixteen."

"Gordon?"

"You can call him Gordie."

"You can call him Pip."

"I have a suggestion: Let's settle this child-naming thing with a contest."

"I'm listening."

"A sort of sexual Olympics," she offers.

"Ooh, I love a challenge. You're going down, woman."

"And so are you. The first event is the sideways sixty-nine sprint to orgasm."

"Huh?"

"The first one to bring the other to orgasm wins."

"Now?"

"Go turn off the stove and grill, and get your butt back up here."

"Italy shall have its first gold medal of this Olympiad," I tease, as I sprint downstairs and turn down the heat. "Dun, DUN-duh, dun dun DUN dun ..."

"That sounds more like 'Rocky' to me."

"Shut it."

I sneak into the Hustler bag and arm myself with the We-Vibe vibrator—dual sensation with penetration. *I can't be defeated.* Bea's already on the bed. I dive next to her and tickle her toes, then remove her panties as she frees Little Mormon from my jeans.

Lovergirl is quite skilled. At this angle, she's able to bury me deep into her throat. I run through baseball statistics to

20

avoid the inevitable. I draw the alphabet and flip on the We-Vibe. *Fuck! I must hurry ... I'm so close!*

Once I have the vibrator in place, she gasps and squeezes my head tightly between her thighs. *Ouch! She's the best chiropractor I ever met.* I hear her muffled ecstasy.

"Oh ... my ... effing ... GOD!" she arches toward climax.

"Booyah, motherfucker," I beam with pride.

She lets loose a thunderous orgasm and finishes me off seconds later. Being the mature type, I do my touchdown dance around the bedroom with my glazed love éclair and purple weapon.

"What is that, and where did you get it?"

"This, Lovergirl, is yet another weapon in my arsenal. Make that Italy one, Canada nil," I bow. "Raise the flag, fuckers! Pippino must be so proud of his poppa."

"You've won the battle, Uncle M, not the war. Now, go finish my dinner."

"Yes, dear."

We laugh through dinner as Bea inspects the bag of badness. I've impressed my love, but I suspect she'll step up her game.

CHAPTER SIX

Opportunity dances with those who are already on the dance floor. – H. Jackson Brown, Jr.

After dinner, we dunk warm Toll House cookies in milk and catch up on *Nurse Jackie* episodes. *Zoey rules!* Bea's appetite—both for food and for sex—is growing, and I'm keeping up, so far.

"One more cookie, Lovergirl. I bet my boy is smiling," I tease as I pat her belly.

"Uncle M, you constantly impress me. You bake?"

"I slaved all night making sure the batter was just right."

"Swoon!"

"Oh, and please ignore the Nestlé bag in the garbage."

"Cheater."

"I need to take it easy, with all those heavy medals soon to be hanging around my neck. My poor back."

"Speaking of, I believe it's time for another event."

"I'll do some deep knee bends and change into my track suit."

"That won't be necessary."

"What's the event?"

"The Grip Test. I noticed two plugs in the bag of fun."

"But ..."

"Exactly."

"Let me chug this wine first." *Gulp* "OK, what are the rules?" I ask as Bea removes the intimidating butt plugs and tube of mint lube from the Hustler bag.

"We each insert one of these and then get it on, missionary-style. Whoever knocks the plug out of the other person's butt, without using hands, wins."

"So embarrassing."

"You can forfeit if you like."

"You may take my pride, but you'll never take my butt plug!"

Lovergirl hands me the plugs and lube, and goes into the kitchen.

"What are you doing?"

"We need this, too," she replies while showing me the pepper shaker.

"Pepper?"

"You'll see, Uncle M."

We disrobe, pull down the comforter, and place two towels on the bed. *Shit. How intimidating!*

"My virgin butt is going to need lots of foreplay, kind words, and a thick layer of lube."

"You can still back out."

"No way. I'm tight, y'all."

Lovergirl lathers the lube onto the plugs and hands me one.

"I don't think I've had anything up there since a thermometer in the sixties."

"Kinky."

"How do we do this? I can't put it in myself," I protest while noticing hers is already in place.

"Gimme."

Yikes!

"Be gentle," I mewl.

She manages to get it in and then mounts me. I concentrate on squeezing my cheeks without pushing as she slams away on top of me.

"Do you like it, Uncle M?"

"It's … different. Stop trying to distract me," I insist.

I bite my bottom lip as she slams harder and harder. All this concentration is delaying my orgasm, so there's one benefit. She orgasms twice, but her plug is cemented; mine is slipping.

Bea covers my eyes and reaches toward the bedside table. *What's she up to?* I hear shaking and, suddenly, I smell pepper.

"Aaaaaah CHOO!" I sneeze, which sends my butt plug flying. *Rats!*

"Bless you."

Canada has her first gold.

CHAPTER SEVEN

Don't let what you cannot do interfere with
what you can do. – John Wooden

It's Bea's big night with her friends. Eric and his partner have been helping plan my surprise. I get the call saying she has left the office, so I drive there. As I pull up, I notice a pickup truck with a large present on wheels in the bed. Eric and Daniel are strapping it down.

"I thought I was jumping out of a cake?" I ask out my Jeep's window.

"The cake was booked, Mormon. This will do just fine," Eric assures me.

"If you say so."

I reach under my passenger seat and extract the second Hustler bag, kept secret from my Lovergirl.

"What have you there?" Daniel asks.

I whip out the Cockasaurus Rex as their eyes light up. I'm not sure if it's envy, arousal, or fear.

"In the words of Otter Stratton, 'She'll take *this* seriously,'" I exclaim while dangling the largest strap-on known to man (or horse, for that matter).

"Oh, my," the boys gasp in stereo.

"Sorry, fellas. Rex is unavailable this evening. He is to ride securely next to my leg, making all the ladies dewy with desire."

"Come inside and try on your outfit, Officer Clydesdale," Daniel suggests.

Why haven't I learned to trust my instincts? Naturally, the police uniform is specifically designed for parades at which I would not dare leave the curb. The pants are faux leather with both ass cheeks cut out. There's matching navy, T-back underwear. The belt contains handcuffs and a whip, not a gun. The shirt pockets have flaps with nipple clamps. A somewhat normal cap and mirrored Ray-Bans are all I have left to hide beneath.

When I emerge from the bathroom to model the costume, Eric and Daniel nearly convulse in laughter.

"Turn around, Mormon."

"No."

"Oh, come on," Daniel encourages.

"I have hair on my ass, Daniel. This won't do."

"We could shave you," suggests Eric.

"Stop, Lover. It's sexy, Mormon," Daniel insists. "Men are supposed to have hair. I see the salami fit perfectly."

"Yum, yum," Eric teases. "Pass the Poupon."

"All right, knock it off before I change my mind. What's the plan?"

Eric informs me that a limo bus is taking the women barhopping downtown, and it will be best to do my thing at the restaurant they're meeting in for Happy Hour. He insists it won't be crowded. Daniel has a Bose wireless speaker linked to an iPod to provide music for my routine.

"Climb into the box and we'll be on our way."

"What? Why can't I ride with you?"

"You'll be seen. Get in. It's only ten miles or so."

"Fine. Fetch thee my tequila for the ride. It's in the bag."

I sit Indian-style in the box. I barely fit. Luckily, the ride isn't too bumpy. When we come to a stop, I lift the top to look around. I see the limo bus. Eric pushes the lid back down.

"Hey! No peeking. You'll be seen."

"Fuck. Fine. Hurry up."

Eric lifts the top a sliver again.

"What?"

"How much of that did you drink?"

"Three fingers, if you must know." I take another pull. "Make that four."

"Stay down until you hear the music begin. Shh."

"Got it."

Eric and Daniel drop the door on the truck bed and lift out the large gift box. They roll me across the parking lot while I take one more swig. Their whispering and giggling is making me nervous. Once inside, I hear various muffled voices.

"Ladies, can I have your attention," Eric begins. "Miss, will you please have a seat right here. Thank you. And now ..."

Joe Cocker's "You Can Leave Your Hat On" begins blaring— my cue to begin. I stand and throw the lid off the box. I hear gasps. *Oh, fuck!* It's a bingo hall filled with senior citizens and seated in the chair in front of me, instead of my Lovergirl, is Grandma Aspinwald.

CHAPTER EIGHT

Love is like dew that falls on both nettles and lilies.
– Swedish Proverb

Normally, I'd be all heels and elbows as I run from the embarrassing situation. However, the tequila has persuaded me to hoard my shits. *Fuck it. I'll dance for the old woman.*

Grandma does a double take, then she recognizes me. The other ladies in the bingo hall begin cheering. I glare at Eric, hop out of the box, and begin gyrating in front of Grandma.

"How did you know it was my birthday, Blobber?" Grandma asks.

"I'm a powerful man with many connections. You shall henceforth address me as Officer Blobber, or I'll be forced to restrain the suspect."

"Eat me," Grandma defies as she gives me the finger and smirks.

"Fine, you asked for it."

I remove the handcuffs from my belt and grab her wrist. *She's enjoying this. Ugh. Maybe it's genetic.*

"You have the right to remain silent. Anything you say won't matter, as I'm going to grind my man banana into the birthday girl anyway," I tease. Grandma giggles as the others in attendance roar. Eric is encouraging me as I notice his partner open the door to the hall. The parade of bachelorette party people stream in, led by my Lovergirl.

Once Grandma is cuffed, I hop in front of her, flip around, squat my hairy butt down onto her lap, and grind.

"Oh, my," Grandma responds. "I hope you registered at Petco so I can buy you shears for your wedding gift."

"Silence, woman, or I shall gag you!"

31

"You wouldn't dare. And, what the hell *is* that thing in your pants? You must be dreaming."

I stand in front or her, then turn and rip my shirt open, sending the buttons flying. I forgot I had my nipples clamped. Good thing I'm numb because I may have just dislocated a gland or two. The women cheer as I do my best impression of a pelvic thrust. By this point, Grandma is in tears laughing. Lovergirl inserts herself between us and begins undoing my belt.

"Oh, Jesus. I wouldn't do that."

"We have to set the beast free, Uncle M," she insists.

She unbuttons, unzips, and yanks down my pants. Out flops the Cockasaurus Rex, which dangles and bops her on the noggin. The women (and gay men) all gasp at the sight of my girthy appendage. I chase the girls in Bea's party around like a kid with a garden hose. Luckily, the song runs out before I get too crazy. I'm dizzy and drunk from all the tequila. Still, I'm confident I've won Grandma over in the process.

"Put that thing away and uncuff me, you maniac," Grandma insists.

"Fuck, I don't have any keys. Sorry, you're stuck. Can you hold a bingo blotter in your mouth?"

"I have the keys, Mormon," Eric offers.

I take a bow and dress myself. I attempt to give Grandma a hug.

"Happy birthday, my dear."

"Thank you and, no, we don't hug. You may fist-tap me."

I oblige. As I turn to leave, Grandma smacks my ass and hugs Bea.

"Was this your doing?" Grandma asks Bea.

"No, it was a surprise to me as well. Eric is responsible."

"Well, let's hope I win a few million dollars tonight. You go have fun at your party."

"I love you, Grandma."

"Love you, too. Keep an eye on this one. He's seems to be a toy short of a Happy Meal."

"Ha! Will do."

Bea leads me out to the limo.

"You're coming with us."

"Oh, hell no. Not like this," I refuse.

"Please."

"I need a fucking nap."

"Just come with us to the bar and you can wait in the limo. I'll sneak out and we'll have a little fun."

"Now *that* sounds tempting."

"I have an idea for the next Olympic event."

"What is it?"

"You'll see."

We pile into the limo. Once downtown, they go into the club as I lie across the seats, hoping to sleep off the tequila buzz. Bea is last to leave. She bends down and kisses me.

"I'll be back in one hour, Uncle M. Make sure that strap-on is ready."

Oh, my.

CHAPTER NINE

Enjoy the little things, for one day you may look back and realize they were the big things. – Robert Brault

I enjoy a much-needed nap, while the limo driver sits in Starbucks reading the newspaper. I'm startled awake by knocking on the limo door. *Probably a homeless dude looking for spare change.* I peek and see that it is Bea, so I push the lever and open the doors. Bea enters with two of her friends.

"What's this? Is the party over already?"

"No, it's just beginning," Bea insists. "These are my friends. I believe you already met Emily."

"Yes, the bartender."

"Indeed. She also happens to be from my home town in Canada."

"Nice."

"And, this is Luca."

"Aw, what a nice name," I compliment as I shake her hand. All three women are tipsy. Something strange is about to happen. I sense it.

"Luca is from Naples."

"Ah, bella!" I respond as I turn her hand over and kiss her knuckles. "Wait a minute. Canadian, Italian: Does this have something to do with our Olympics?"

"Yes, it does. These fine ladies are occasional lovers ..."

"Yes! Oops. I mean, oh, how interesting."

"... and they have agreed to participate in our next event. Uncle M, you will be coaching Luca and I will coach Emily."

"All right. Is this the javelin toss?"

"Close. I'm going to need that strap on," Bea informs as she begins undoing my pants again. "Here's how this works:

Each participant will take turns strapping on Rex here. The other will be on the receiving end. The one who takes in the most length wins."

"Ha! Impossible!"

Bea removes Cockasaurus Rex from my waist and holds it out. It's huge. No human could ever...

Luca takes Rex from Bea and sneers, "You're going to need a bigger dildo."

"That's my girl."

We turn on Timberlake, dim the lights, and ring the bell. First up is Emily. Luca straps the beast on while Emily lifts her skirt and removes her thong. She conveniently has a tube of Astroglide in her purse, which she applies liberally. Lovergirl sits next to me as we watch the first attempt. The women kneel. Luca holds steady while Emily backs into her.

"There's just no way," I insist.

"Come on, Emily. You can do it."

Luca slides the tip up and down Emily's hungry slit. *If she can take the head alone, I'll be impressed.* Emily arches, lowers her shoulders, and pushes back into Luca. The entire head enters. Emily's face shows pleasure, not pain, as does Luca's. Luca pulls out a bit and pushes in farther. Emily cringes and gets another inch in, and another, and another. *What a trooper, eh?*

"That's it, Emily. Oh, Can-nuh-daaaah ...," Bea sings.

Emily is able to stuff in another inch before she's "full." Luca smirks while Emily dismounts and unstraps. Bea takes Rex and surveys the damage.

"Fucking impressive," I admit.

Bea marks the progress with her lip gloss. The thing is as big as my fist and she got a good six-plus inches in. Italy is doomed.

Emily straps on the beast and glazes some fresh lube on as Luca removes her jeans and panties. She has a quiet, confident look. Luca kneels in front of Emily, doggie-style as well. Emily presses the head against Luca's glistening pussy. Her lips part and she takes the head.

"Yes! Do it," I encourage.

Luca grimaces as she takes inch after inch, but she's an inch shy of the mark, and Rex is bending.

"Hold Rex still, Emily. Come on, Luca."

"No, I can't. It's ... just ... too ... big."

"Are you giving up?" Bea asks, but I interrupt.

"Don't you dare! You can do this, Luca," I encourage as Luca gives me an exasperated glance. "Use the force, Luca."

Luca lowers her chest to the floor, breathes quickly like a woman in labor, and pushes back, taking that final inch plus another for good measure.

Italy 2, Canada 1.

CHAPTER TEN

The human heart feels things the eyes cannot see, and knows what the mind cannot understand. – Robert Valett

I want to spend the night before the wedding with Bea, but she resists due to that crazy custom about seeing the bride on the day of the ceremony. I text to convince her otherwise.

Mormon Silver: I'm going to cook the love of my life dinner and cater to her needs, no matter what day or time it is.
Bea Plastique: You're not seeing me after midnight until I walk the beach into your arms forever.
Mormon Silver: Wow!
Bea Plastique: Not a minute past midnight, Mister.
Mormon Silver: Seriously?
Bea Plastique: It's bad luck.
Mormon Silver: It is not. Come on. I have a wonderful night planned.
Bea Plastique: You have me until 11:59.
Mormon Silver: OK, we'll see. Come over at 7 for dinner. How does Chicken Saltimbocca sound?
Bea Plastique: Delish.

When she arrives, I have the table set, candles lit, dinner simmering, honey-butter rolls browning, and Sinatra singing. I also have one more handy ditty I picked up at Hustler: a blindfold. Bea greets me with a kiss and a bottle of my favorite wine: Silver Oak.

"Honey, you didn't have to bring anything. Let's save this until we can have it together."

"Doctor says Gordie and I can have a glass of wine with dinner, no problem," she insists while she pats her little belly.

"OK, *one* glass with Pippino. After dinner, I have a special dessert planned. It's going to require that you wear this," I instruct as I show her the argyle blindfold.

"Ooh, sexy! I can't wait."

While dining, we chat about tomorrow's ceremony and timing. We agreed to have something intimate with immediate family and close friends only.

"Are you ready, Lovergirl?"

"You bet."

"Give me ten minutes to get things ready upstairs. Be right back."

I fill the tub in my master bath and light vanilla candles around it. I float rose petals and add scented bath salts. I have Bea's favorite shampoo, body wash, and two loofah gloves ready. I undress, put on a robe, and return downstairs to Bea.

"OK, first you need to put this on," I inform her as I place the blindfold over her eyes with the strap under her hair. "Come with me." I lead her upstairs. Once in my bedroom, I continue, "Now, let's get you out of these clothes." I kiss her, neck to toes, while undressing her. "I don't want you to have any stress about tomorrow. Everything will be perfect, my love."

Once naked, I lead her to the tub. The water is trickling, and the scent is exotic. I guide her in slowly. I have a tray of chocolate-covered cake pops for snacking.

"Now, I'm going to wash your hair and give you a scalp massage."

"Seems I picked the right man after all."

"Yes, you have."

I wash and rinse her hair, while feeding her bites of cake pops—red velvet, lemon, vanilla, and fudge.

"Ahh. I could take a nap now."

"Not yet, Lovergirl. Scoot up and make room for Uncle M."

I slide into the tub behind her, rub her neck and shoulders, and bathe her slowly with the loofah gloves. We top the session off with a water-sloshing lovemaking session. After soaking in our orgasmic bliss, I get out of the tub while asking her to stay. I retrieve two warm towels from my laundry room and use them to dry my love.

I honor her desires, and walk my wife-to-be out to her car with thirty minutes to spare. Taped to her driver's side door is a gray tie, a calling card from Chris. *Too late, buddy. She's all mine.*

CHAPTER ELEVEN

No man is truly married until he understands every word his wife is NOT saying. – Anonymous

Wedding Day—the happiest day of a person's life, right next to that first taste of Nutella. Eric picks me up, and we make our way downtown to the Hotel Del Coronado. Bea and I will exchange vows on the beach in front of the historic hotel where *Some Like it Hot* was filmed with Marilyn Monroe.

I'm wearing a black tux with the pants tied off at my knees. I have my signature silver argyle socks beneath them. Who knows what Bea will wear? She's eccentric to say the least, and Eric won't share, although I pry.

"Will you at least tell me the color?"

"Not telling you. Mormon, take my word for it. She'll look fabulous."

"Hey, do we have time for a quick Mojito to calm the nerves?"

"Now we're talking."

Eric detours off the highway and we stop at Poseidon in Del Mar—the masters of the Mojito. In a few sips, my nerves are calm.

Once we arrive at the Hotel Del, I check in at the front desk. They have our honeymoon suite ready. Bea is there having the final touches applied. Guests are gathering by the pool in the afternoon sun, sipping Prosecco. I see my mother chatting with Grandma. I approach them.

"Hello, Ms. A, I see you've met my mother." I greet my mother with a kiss on the cheek. She looks elegant in her powder blue dress. "How was your flight?"

"It was quick, thanks to my Kindle. I finished two books."

"Well done."

"How's your writing coming along?" Mother asks.

"You know," Grandma interrupts, "you should be proud of your son. He's quite a talented blogger."

"Why, thank you, Ms. A. I wasn't aware that you read my blog."

"I enjoy it immensely." Grandma grabs my mother's arm. "He's also an amazing dancer."

Right. Maybe when I'm blotto on tequila and have a third leg strapped to me.

"Really?" my mother reacts.

"You're too kind."

The wedding coordinator directs us all out to the platform on the beach. *It's time.* Other hotel guests come to the edge of the resort to watch.

I take my position next to the Justice. A guitar soloist begins the "Bridal March" song. The guests rise and turn to see the bride. iPhone pictures are snapping away. I see the doors open and catch my first glimpse of Lovergirl. She's escorted by Eric. Her hair is shorter and she's wearing the famous Marilyn Monroe dress worn over the air vent in *The Seven Year Itch.*

Wow!

My eyes water with delight. She's stunning. Eric hands her off to me, and we begin the quick ceremony. We exchange vows we've written for each other, slide rings over fingers, and share our first kiss as wife and husband. Our guests applaud as we turn and wave.

Suddenly, there's a commotion on the beach. Two military Jeeps approach and stop at the base of the platform. A helicopter appears and begins circling above us.

"What's this?" I ask Bea.

"I'm not sure, but I have an idea who it might be."

As the helicopter approaches, blowing sand, I notice a name written on the side: Chunky Salsa, or something. *Who names his fucking bird? Only the most pretentious of asses.* The copter lands, and Chris emerges with a bodyguard. They approach us. The bodyguard hands an envelope to Bea as I glare at Chris.

"Ma'am, this is a wedding gift from my boss."

She opens it and reads the notice within, as she turns pale.

"What is it?"

"An eviction notice. Chris bought the Hyatt. I have ten days to move."

CHAPTER TWELVE

Our greatest glory is not in never falling, but in rising every time we fall. – Confucius

"May I see that?" I request. Bea hands me the notice. I look at it briefly, then sneeze into it, and crumble it like a tissue. "I'm sorry, I'm allergic to fuckwads. Now, if you wouldn't mind, the missus and I have a life to attend to—a life with lots of love, sex, and children, regardless of our financial situation."

Chris smirks at me, then he and his bodyguard leave. Grandma and Eric are first to console Bea.

"Honey, I'm so sorry," Grandma explains. "I tried everything to block him, but we're too far behind and the bank insisted."

"At least we'll have the proceeds from the sale, right?" Bea asks.

"Actually, there *are* no proceeds. It was a short sale," Grandma laments. "I'm being tossed out as well. We'll both be homeless for a bit."

"Nobody's going to be homeless. I have plenty of room at my place. I'd be honored to have two guests to try my recipes on."

"He does make a mean French toast," Grandma remarks.

"I'll prepare a chore list for each of you, and we'll discuss your allowances."

Bea smiles, finally.

"Hey, let's deal with this tomorrow," I suggest. "It will work out."

"I know, husband. Eric and I have been working on a project that should solve this predicament," Bea recovers.

"Husband. I like the sound of that, wife," I assure Bea. I hold her face between my hands, wipe the tears with my thumbs, and kiss her. "Let's save what's left of the day and have fun with our guests."

The sunset reception is wonderful, but Chris floats around the back of my mind. When I visit the bar to freshen my bourbon, Eric joins me.

"So, Eric, tell me about this project you're working on."

"Not yet, Mormon. We need a few more commitments. You'll be blown away, if we can pull this off."

"Well, let me know if there's anything I can do to help."

"I will."

"I don't want my expectant wife to stress over this."

"Agreed. She's a strong woman. She'll be fine."

"Cool. What are you drinking?"

"Lemon drop."

"Refreshing!"

When we sit for dinner, I tease Bea about her dress.

"That was a great fucking idea, right there. You have no idea the butterflies you gave me when you came through that door."

"Aw. I'm so glad you like it."

"We do need to find an air vent, though, so we can have the true Marilyn effect."

"Hm, can't do that."

"Why not?"

"I'm not wearing underwear."

"None?"

"Nope."

"Not even a thong?"

"Commando," she insists as she slides my hand from her knee to her sexiness.

"Here comes the bride ... again," I tease.

We agree to postpone our honeymoon until after we deal with the move. There must be a way to extract Chris from our lives. Our wedding night in the suite is memorable and exhausting. Although the bed is cushy, Lovergirl insists we do it on a wooden chair because "we haven't done that yet." I'll never say no to love, regardless of the playing surface. Still, my sore ass wishes I would be more discerning.

CHAPTER THIRTEEN

Don't walk in front of me, I may not follow. Don't walk behind me, I may not lead. Just walk beside me and be my friend forever. – George Fox

It was a difficult night to sleep through with the crazy wedding day we had. Bea is up before me, as usual. She pokes me with a hockey stick to wake me.

"Hey!"

"Get out of bed, husband. We're going to the Ice Arena. I need to blow off some steam."

"Did you just poke me with a stick?"

She jabs me again.

"Let's go. Move it!"

"Jesus. Really? And, why do you have a hockey stick with you here, in our honeymoon suite?"

"I don't leave home without it."

"Ugh."

I drag my groggy butt out from under the soft sheets, and slide into board shorts, flip flops, and a T-shirt.

"Ready."

"You're going to skate in that?"

"It's all I have. I wasn't planning on a morning on ice."

"OK, then."

We jump into the Jeep and head to the skating arena. I hate ice skating because I suck at it. In fact, I can't think of anything I suck at that I enjoy. That's why I hate golf too: I suck at it, I don't want to invest the time to suck less, so I don't golf. Well, this is marriage. A man has to learn to compromise, or he's going to ride a lonely sofa into the sunset.

At the arena, we strap on skates. Yes, I look ridiculous and I'm half asleep so I don't fucking care.

"Why do we need hockey sticks?" I ask, fearing the worst.

"It's time for Olympic event number four. Canada needs a boost, and I'm pretty confident we can even the medal count with this event."

"All right, hoser, bring it! I predict Italy clinches the series this morning."

We carry our sticks out to the ice. Bea reaches behind the boards, grabs two pucks, and flips them out onto the ice.

"Now what?" I ask while stretching my hamstrings, which ache in anticipation.

"We race around the arena. The first one to skate with the puck around each net three times wins."

"Can't we just have sex in the penalty box or something?"

"Maybe."

"Yes! I forfeit."

"Not so fast. If you beat me, we'll do it in the penalty box."

"You hear that, Pippino? Daddy's getting lucky on ice again."

"Ready? Set? Go!"

She takes off. I manage to fall on my face in two strides. I struggle back to my feet, as I see Bea's lovely butt wiggle, while she kicks up ice shavings. *I'm hosed.* Before I make it around the first net, she has already cleared the second and is threatening to lap me. She catches me in no time and knocks my stick from my hands as she passes me. Players make it look so easy: You drop your stick, you bend over, you pick it up, you keep skating. I bend over and fall. I get up on one knee, grab the stick, get up, and fall backward, as she approaches to pass me again.

This time I hold my stick tightly. I make it halfway to the second net as she scoots by, throwing a hip into me, which sends the stick and me flying. She steals my puck and fires it into the net behind me as she whips around the final time. I helplessly sit on my clumsy ass as she finishes the third lap and slides to a halt, spraying me with an ice shower from her skates.

"Canada two, Italy two."

"Feel better?" I ask, as I crawl to the boards, and pull myself up.

"I do actually."

"OK. Now let's get out of here and figure out what we're going to do about this Chris situation."

"Not so fast. Get in that penalty box, mister. I'm not done blowing off steam."

Sometimes the silver isn't so bad.

Molto bene!

CHAPTER FOURTEEN

People with goals succeed because they know where they are going. — Earl Nightingale

We manage to move most of Bea's and Grandma's belongings into storage, except some knickknacks and furniture they insist upon to make my place less of a bachelor pad. They also request I remove the plastic fruit and stop using my kitchen nook as a giant mailbox.

"What's this contraption?" Grandma asks as she and Bea survey my space.

"A foosball table. Wanna play?"

"I think it would look better in the garage," Bea suggests.

"Oh, definitely," Grandma agrees. "This space needs an antique chaise lounge with a side table and decorative lamp."

"Fine. Can I at least keep the poker table?"

"Well," Bea considers, "perhaps we could make use of that."

The three of us catch *Fox 5 News* while sipping our morning stimulant. The special guest they have on this morning is none other than his dickiness, Chris.

Host: How are your renovations coming along?
Chris: We're nearly finished with the first phase. As you know, I was the chief architect on the guestroom redesign back in January, and now that I own the building, I plan to return the site to the splendor it once was. The Grey Towers will once again be the crown jewel of San Diego.
Host: That's exciting.
Chris: Indeed. We're making the resort more family friendly as well. If I may, I'd like to invite your viewers to

an open house and ribbon cutting event we're hosting on Friday. Bring the kids, as we'll have a bounce house and other fun activities for them. There will be tours of the redesigned suites and pool deck, and complementary beverages.

A light bulb, while slightly dim in my advanced years, sparks to life in my mind.

"Ugh, he's disgusting," Bea reacts.

"Say, do either of you have any contacts at Fox?" I ask.

"I think Eric is good friends with one of their reporters, Matt," Bea suggests.

"Perfect. See if Eric can put me in touch with him. I have an idea."

"Let's hear it," Grandma insists.

"Let me hash it out a bit more, then I'll run it by you both. Oh, I also need a clown costume."

"You're scaring me," Bea laughs.

"Good!"

Bea leaves for the office, and Grandma visits the farmer's market while I write a few more blog entries and work on my plan of vengeance. I call my buddy, Jeff.

"Dude, do you still coach that Little League team?" I ask.

"Yep."

"What ages?"

"Eleven and twelve."

"Perfect. I'm going to rent a bus and take the team to the open house of the former Hyatt. I'll try to get my new pal, Trevor Hoffman, to speak."

"Sounds fun. When is it?"

"Friday at six. Let's all meet at the La Costa Park and Ride at five."

"I'll start contacting parents."

"Excellent."

That arrogant prick is going down.

CHAPTER FIFTEEN

Shoot for the moon. Even if you miss, you'll land among the stars. — Les Brown

On the day of my uprising, I pick up my clown costume, makeup, and a large banner. I take it all to Bea's office so she can put my face on. Eric greets me as I enter.

"How are you, Mormon?"

"Insanity in progress, and today should prove it. Make sure you watch the news tonight. Did you get in contact with Matt from Fox?"

"You bet. Here's his mobile. He said to text him when ready."

"You are the man, Eric."

"... but, I'll play the woman, occasionally."

"TMI."

"Something looks different on you. Have you lost weight?"

"I shaved."

"Ah, sexy."

"Thank you."

Bea greets me and we go into her office. *Ah, this is where the lovin' started.*

"OK, baby face, what are you up to?" she asks.

"I'd rather not say. This way, if my plot blows up, you won't be implicated. But, if this goes as planned, Chris will get his comeuppance."

"Ooh, you said 'come.'"

"Behave. I need you to put this clown makeup on my face."

"Hm, never had sex with a clown."

"All right. Do this and my red nose and I will fuck you silly."

"Yes!"

Bea does a great job making my face match my maniacal thoughts. Naturally, she mounts me the second I finish putting on the costume.

"Leave that zipper down, Uncle M. You promised."

"All aboard, Lovergirl," I demand.

The clown outfit is ridiculous: over-sized, white shoes, silver argyle socks, a black and white jumpsuit rolled up to my knees, a silver wig, and a black top hat. I hope I don't cause any accidents on the way downtown.

When I arrive at the Park & Ride, most of the kids are already there, playing catch in the parking lot. I'm wisely armed with candy, which I hand out while greeting the kids. My friend, Jeff, doesn't recognize me.

"Hi, did Mormon hire ... oh, Jesus."

"What do you think?"

"You have completely lost your mind."

"Oh, you haven't seen anything yet," I tease while I honk my toy horn.

The limo bus arrives and we climb aboard with fourteen kids all hyped up on sugar. We sing, dance, and tell fart jokes on the way to the Grey Towers. I send a text to Matt from Fox as we pull up.

Mormon: Hey, Matt. Please meet us on the second parking level underground. Look for the black limo bus.
Matt: On our way.
Mormon: Will you be able to use a live feed from there?
Matt: Won't be a problem.
Mormon: Excellent.

When we arrive, I ask the kids to wait in the bus while I open the fun house. I pull the banner from my bag and stick it to the wall. It reads, "Grey's Funhouse," and has a big arrow, which points to the doorway. I pull out my iPhone and cross my fingers as I click the link. I hear the buzzing and unlatching. *Yes!* I open the door to the Blue Room.

"Come on in, kids!"

CHAPTER SIXTEEN

We must walk consciously only part way toward our goal
and then leap in the dark to our success.
– Henry David Thoreau

As Chris leads the press conference and ribbon cutting in the lobby, I turn the kids loose on the Blue Room. I remove certain DVDs and put baseball on all the TVs, to soften the blow. The kids play on the swings, whack each other with dildos, squirt lube on the floor, and slide around. The Fox News van pulls up.

Chris is bragging on camera about the remodel and how family-friendly the resort has become. Meanwhile, the *Fox News* team reports from the Blue Room where Matt interviews the evil clown.

"My Lord. What's going on here?" Matt asks.

"Wow, I have no idea. We were told to bring the kids down for some family fun. This is just awful. Did you see the crazy devices in this room?"

"It looks like a BDSM dungeon."

"I know! Disgusting."

I walk with Matt around the Blue Room while Jeff gathers the kids and takes them upstairs for refreshments.

"Look at this paddle," I prompt, as I remove it from its wall mount. The camera zooms in.

"There's a plaque on it. Hm, CG. I wonder who that is?" Matt asks.

"Oh, I think we both know, Matt," I say as I wink at the camera. "Now, I have to get back to the kids and make sure they're OK."

Matt continues his broadcast as I go into the limo bus and change out of my clown costume. I hide it in a compartment under the seats and begin removing my makeup. A text comes in.

Bea Plastique: OMFG!!!
Mormon Silver: What?
Bea Plastique: I'm watching this live with Grandma.
Mormon Silver: They say TV adds ten pounds. Did I look chubby?
Bea Plastique: Chris just broke away from the ceremony. He's on his way there.
Mormon Silver: Got it handled. TTYL

I put on my baseball cap and sunglasses, and walk casually past the media as they rush toward the Blue Room. Chris and his entourage are close behind them. He doesn't recognize me either. When he gets to the door, I yell toward him.

"Yo, Chris."

He pivots and sees me.

"Love what you've done to the place. Have a nice life, fuckhead," I yell, give him the finger, and jog out of the garage.

I text Jeff, asking him to take care of getting the kids back north and to keep mum about my involvement. I take a taxi home. Bea and Grandma are waiting.

"Holy shit," Grandma beams, "you are one twisted motherfucker."

"Language!" Bea reacts.

"I can't believe he didn't change the code. How's he spinning it?" I ask.

"He stuttered and stammered, saying he never knew about the room," Bea informs me.

"But, when Matt asked him about the paddle he completely lost it and ran off camera," Grandma continues.

The media had a field day with the scandal. Jeff played it perfectly, insisting he had no idea what was going on as he simply followed the banner. Chris will be tied up for some time doing damage control. This should give my wife and I time to prepare for our child, with fewer distractions.

CHAPTER SEVENTEEN

*Love is the expansion of two natures in such fashion that
each include the other, each is enriched by the other.*
– Felix Adler

I'm home finishing more blog entries, hoping they drive
revenue to help me catch up on the mortgage. Grandma
leaves for Canada to visit family for a few days, so Bea and I
have the house to ourselves.

**Bea Plastique: I say we have the final event in our baby
naming Olympics tonight. You game?**
Mormon Silver: Sure. What do you have in mind?
**Bea Plastique: Strip Poker. Do you know how to play
Texas hold 'em?**
**Mormon Silver: Never heard of it. Does it involve steer
wrestling?**
Bea Plastique: You're not bluffing me, mister.
Mormon Silver: Bring it, sister!

I'm not bluffing, as my card skills are nearly as bad as my
skating skills. I don't even know if a straight beats a flush.
Still, I won't back down from a challenge.

The key to strip poker (*I Googled it*) is to have many items
to remove. Hence, I enter our walk-in closet and begin
layering up. I find Bea's purple thong and make it my first
item. If nothing else, it should distract her. Then I add boxer
briefs and jeans. I create makeshift pasties out of electrical
tape in the form of crosses over my nipples. I put on a tank
top, T-shirt, polo shirt, button-down, and a scarf. I add socks
and Pumas, then a bandana, cap, and sunglasses. *No way
she wins.*

When Bea arrives home, I'm a sweaty mess.

"Is there a cold front coming in?"

"Get your cute little ass over to the poker table. Italy shall claim the crown tonight."

"Fine. I'm going to change first. Start shuffling, Uncle M."

When she comes back downstairs, all she's wearing is a sundress and sandals.

"That's it?"

"This is all I need," she insists. "Can I get you a drink while I'm up? Bourbon, perhaps?"

"Yes ... hold on. No drugging me."

"I'd never."

"Right. Bring me the sealed bottle and a glass, Miss Thang."

"As you wish."

We begin our event. I lose hand after hand after hand. I'm two bourbons in and down to pasties and underwear. Bea laughs when she sees the black crosses over my nipples.

"What were you thinking? Did you forget you have chest hair?"

"Um ..."

"You lose this hand and I get to remove them."

"Fine."

I lose the hand. She removes them like Band-Aids and leaves me with two pink, tender-skinned crosses. Bea is in her bra and panties. I finally get a favorable draw, win the hand, and off comes her bra.

"Looks like a dead heat," I remark.

"Not quite."

Bea wins the next hand and assumes she's the victor until I peel down my boxer briefs and model her thong.

68

"That has to be one of the most disturbing things I've ever seen," Bea laughs as she tries to snap a picture with her iPhone. "I'm posting this on Facebook."

"Give me that," I insist, as I take the phone from her.

On the next hand I learn that a straight does not beat a flush; I have a flush.

"Yes! Italy wins!"

"Hold on, Uncle M," Bea interrupts as she peels down her panties to reveal a silver chain coming from her luscious love tunnel.

"What the heck is that?"

"The chain to my Ben Wa balls."

"Fuck."

Bea wins the next hand, once again confident in Canada's victory.

"Heck no. This fat lady ain't singin' yet," I insist as I turn around, peel down the thong, and expose the silver hoop dangling from my crack. It's Ben Wa balls versus anal beads for the title.

CHAPTER EIGHTEEN

Kisses that are easily obtained are easily forgotten.
– English Proverb

Poker is a funny game, especially when you have beads in the bum. Perhaps that distraction was causing my string of losses to Lovergirl, but after seeing what's dangling from me, she's straining to see her cards through tearing eyes.

I'm dealt Ace-King, and do as I should: go all in. The flop is Ace-King-Deuce. If this were on ESPN, I'd see that exciting number saying I have something like a 99% chance of winning this hand. Bea foolishly goes all in also. She has more chips than I do, so this is a critical hand.

"Oh, Lovergirl. You're going down. Let's see what you have."

"No."

"Those are the rules. Flip them."

"No. Not until all five cards are out. I want to watch you sweat."

Jesus. Does she have pocket Aces?

The next two cards turned are off-suit Eight and Four. I have a sure winner. I flip my cards over and rejoice that I can name our child, yank her chain, and lose my string of butt-pearls. She bites her lip and turns over her cards: a pair of Deuces. *Fuck me in the eyehole.*

"Are you kidding me, woman?"

"Oh, Can-nuh-daaah," she sings while doing her happy dance.

"How the hell do you win a hand with Deuces?"

"Let's go, Uncle M," she insists as she leads me upstairs. "It's time for the removal of the final item. You don't mind if

I drape my nation's flag over my shoulders while performing, do you?"

In my candlelit bedroom, Lovergirl sits up on the bed while I lie between her legs with my chin propped on my hands—an eager spectator. She slowly removes the Ben Wa balls with her left hand while circling her clit with the fingertips of her right. *I love watching my woman touch herself.* I'm bone-hard between the varied sensations including the yellow pill I took before our poker match.

Every time I try to assist in her pleasure, she raises a foot to my forehead and pushes me back.

"I want you to sit up facing me," she suggests, "and touch yourself too, Uncle M."

"All right."

Mutual masturbation is a first for me. When I'm ready to erupt, she reaches toward me to (I assume) give me a hand. Instead, as my Mormon-juice rises, she yanks the beads from me as if she were starting a leaf blower.

"Eek," is all I can manage. I feel violated—in a good way. "Great, now what do we do with the beads?"

"I think they're dishwasher safe," she offers.

"Yuck! Why don't we keep them in a bedside jar of barbicide?"

"Ha!"

The next morning, Grandma arrives home as we finish breakfast.

"Welcome home, Grandmother," I greet her. "French toast?"

"Yum. Yes, please."

"Hello, darling," Grandma greets Bea.

"How was your trip?"

"Very productive. It's a done deal."

"What's a done deal?" I interrupt.

"The three of us and Eric are going to Comic-Con tomorrow."

"Cool, I always wanted to check that out."

"Good," Bea beams.

"We're meeting the group at nine," says Grandma.

"What group?"

"You'll see."

CHAPTER NINETEEN

Once in awhile, right in the middle of an ordinary life, love gives us a fairy tale. – Anonymous

We drive down to Comic-Con. I'm amazed by the variety of outfits and personalities. Crowds gather in bunches around celebrity sightings. Grandma hands out VIP badges as the limo drops us off at the main entrance.

"I like how you travel, woman."

"The meeting is in Room 19 on the Mezzanine Level," Grandma informs us.

"What meeting?" I ask.

"Ooh, Mormon, you're going to love this," Eric assures me.

A concierge guides us through the crowd and up the escalator to the Mezzanine. We stop at the concession counter to grab coffee. I take Bea aside.

"What's going on, sweetie?"

"Eric and I have been working this deal for months. Grandma made some contacts, and it all came together beautifully."

"So, she wasn't in Canada last week?"

"She was in Hollywood."

"Why?"

"You'll see."

"They're ready for you, folks," the concierge informs us. "Right this way."

My palms are sweaty and my mouth is dry. What could this be? I turn the corner into the room and see a small group of executive-looking people behind a conference room table containing various documents and pens. The flat-screen TV in front of the table has a web browser. It's on the home page of my blog.

I stare at Bea, still confused.

"Mormon, these folks are from Macmillan," Grandma introduces.

I press palms with various executives from the publishing giant, then Grandma leads me over to another gentleman.

"I believe you know this fellow," Grandma suggests as he smiles and shakes my hand.

"Mark Fucking Wahlberg?" I gasp.

"Mark Robert Michael Wahlberg, actually," he corrects me.

"Jesus. Sorry, dude. I'm a huge fan," I offer, while holding his handshake uncomfortably long.

"As am I, Mormon. I've been reading your blog for weeks. You have quite a story."

"I apologize. Can someone tell me what's going on here?"

Bea grabs both my hands and stares me in the eyes.

"Darling, Macmillan is offering a three-book deal and Mr. Wahlberg would like to option the film rights ... for five million dollars."

I nearly faint.

"All that's left is the signing of the agreements. Our attorney has reviewed them. Congratulations, my love."

Bea kisses me. I'm blown away, elated, and humbled. I've been blogging about my bizarre relationship with Lovergirl since that first meeting in her office. I never intended to publish it.

"Books and a movie? About us?"

"Let's say, *inspired by* us."

"You can change some of the facts, you know, to protect the innocent," Mark suggests.

"Start by changing the names," Bea insists.

I sign the documents, stare at the advance checks, and pinch myself. Once home, I sit in front of my computer...

My name is ~~Mormon Silver~~ Phil Torcivia, and women leave their marks on me.

THE END.

CHAPTER TWENTY (EPILOGUE)

A man is given the choice between loving women and understanding them. – Ninon de L'Enclos

I'm at Poinsettia Park, playing catch with my lovely daughter, Gerty. She's an all-star junior in high school, and one of the best pitchers in the nation. Her sister, Dee, is in the on-deck circle, hovering over a tripod while focusing a high-speed camera.

WHAPPP

"Ouch! Take it easy on the old man, will ya?"

"Oh, Dad."

"Seriously. I'm not wearing a cup. Straight stuff only."

ZZZIP

Dee's camera clicks off numerous shots with every pitch. I take a quick water break.

"I thought twins were supposed to be alike. You should be catching your sister."

"Sports are silly, except for their artistic qualities," she responds while showing me an action photo on the camera.

"Nice."

"We need about a dozen more good ones for the yearbook."

"Great. I'm going to need a thicker glove."

As I head back behind the plate, Bea is sitting in the stands smiling at me.

"How are you holding up?"

"I'm fine."

"Could be worse. You could have a son throwing in the nineties."

"Good point and, just so you know, I'm not opposed to having another go at my little Pippino."

"That will be up to your daughters. Better start working on them now."

"Grandson Pippino. *Perfecto!*"

I put the catcher's mask on and squat.

"OK, baby doll. Let her fly."

"Pop?"

"Yes."

BZZZT

"I've been kind of seeing someone, and he asked if I'd go to the Senior Prom with him."

"You've been seeing him or *seeing* him?"

"Ugh. You know."

"No, and I'm not sure I want to."

"Whatever."

SSSNAP

"Anyway, he's a nice guy. He plays baseball."

"All right, that's one good thing."

"He got accepted to Stanford."

"Two. Does he treat you like a lady?"

"Of course. In fact just yesterday he gave me a romantic gift."

"Flowers?"

"No, a butt plug," she winks.

FFFFFT, BOINK, CRACK ... sinkerball, square in the nuts.

ABOUT THE AUTHOR

Please join the fun by following my rants at Torcivia.com, Facebook.com/SuchaNiceGuy, and Twitter.com/PhilTorcivia.

My books, available in paperback and e-book formats:
- *Such a Nice Guy* (October 2009)
- *Still a Nice Guy* (April 2010)
- *Nice Meeting You* (October 2010)
- *Just a Nice Guy* (April 2011)
- *What a Nice Guy* (September 2011)
- *Nice Knowing You* (February 2012)
- *The 10/60 Diet: How to lose 10% of your body weight in 60 days.* (May 2011)
- *Fifty Shades of Silver Hair and Socks* (May 2012)
- *Fifty Shades Shadier* (June 2012)
- *Fifty Shades Effed* (July 2012)
- *Have a Nice Guy* (September 2012)

9 781478 172864